SAVING THE ENDANGERED
AMERICAN ALLIGATOR

JEANNE NAGLE

Britannica®
Educational Publishing

IN ASSOCIATION WITH

ROSEN
EDUCATIONAL SERVICES

Published in 2016 by Britannica Educational Publishing (a trademark of Encyclopædia Britannica, Inc.) in association with The Rosen Publishing Group, Inc.
29 East 21st Street, New York, NY 10010

Distributed exclusively by Rosen Publishing.

To see additional Britannica Educational Publishing titles, go to rosenpublishing.com.

First Edition

Britannica Educational Publishing
J.E. Luebering: Director, Core Reference Group
Mary Rose McCudden: Editor, Britannica Student Encyclopedia

Rosen Publishing
Heather Moore Niver: Editor
Nelson Sá: Art Director
Michael Moy: Designer
Cindy Reiman: Photography Manager
Heather Moore Niver: Photo Researcher

Library of Congress Cataloging-in-Publication Data

Nagle, Jeanne, author.
  Saving the endangered American alligator / Jeanne Nagle.
    pages cm. — (Conservation of endangered species)
  Includes bibliographical references and index.
  Audience: Grades 1 to 4.
  ISBN 978-1-68048-252-2 (library bound) — ISBN 978-1-5081-0057-7 (pbk.) — ISBN 978-1-68048-310-9 (6-pack)
  1. American alligator—Juvenile literature. 2. American alligator—Conservation—Juvenile literature. I. Title.
  QL666.C925N34 2016
  597.98'4—dc23
                                                                                              2015017788

Manufactured in the United States of America

Photo Credits: Cover Juan Gracia/Shutterstock.com; back cover, p. 1, interior pages background FloridaStock/Shutterstock.com; p. 4 Danita Delimont/Gallo Images/Getty Images; p. 5 © iStockphoto.com/tswinner; pp. 6, 8 Hope Lourie Killcoyne; p. 7 Encyclopaedia Britannica, Inc.; p. 9 © iStockphoto.com/atlanticcoastphotography; p. 10 Jim Abernethy/National Geographic Image Collection/Getty Images; p. 11 Heiko Kiera/Shutterstock.com; p. 12 tristan tan/Shutterstock.com; p. 13 © iStockphoto.com/Whirler; p. 14 Tim Chapman/Hulton Archive/Getty Images; p. 15 Mark Ralston/AFP/Getty Images; p. 16 Miami Herald/Tribune News Service/Getty Images; p. 17 Willard R. Culver/National Geographic Image Collection/Getty Images; p. 18 Wirepec/iStock/Thinkstock; p. 19 David Tipling/Lonely Planet Images/Getty Images; p. 20 © iStockphoto.com/ehrlif; p. 21 Guido Blandon/AFP/Getty Images; p. 22 Don Johnston/All Canada Photos/Getty Images; p. 23 © iStockphoto.com/Alex Potemkin; p. 24 Philippe Henry/Oxford Scientific/Getty Images; p. 25 Clark Wheeler/E+/Getty Images; p. 26 Carlton Ward/ National Geographic Image Collection/Getty Images; p. 27 billybruce2000/iStock/Thinkstock; p. 28 Bildagentur Zoonar GmbH/Shutterstock.com; p. 29 © iStockphoto.com/lathuric; cover and interior pages design elements Ellika/Shutterstock.com (alligator silhouette), Ekaterina Pokrovsky/Shutterstock.com (alligator skin)

CONTENTS

ALLIGATORS IN THE WILD

Alligators, or gators as they are also called, have fascinated people for a long time. Some people have even tried to keep them as pets. They soon found out that was not a good idea, however. Alligators are large and dangerous animals that should live in the wild.

Being taken out of the wild is one reason

Adult alligators are long and large—and they do not make good house pets.

4

Vocabulary

Endangered species are plants and animals that are in danger of disappearing forever.

why American alligators became an **endangered species.** Other reasons were overhunting and a loss of the places gators call home.

In the 1960s, the United States government and caring individuals realized that alligators were in danger of dying out. Steps were taken to save them. Today, American alligators are no longer endangered. The story of how gators were saved may help endangered animals in the future.

When resting underwater, only the alligator's eyes and nose can be seen.

TYPES OF ALLIGATORS

Alligators belong to the group of animals called reptiles. A reptile is an air-breathing animal that has scales on the outside of its body instead of hair or feathers. Lizards, turtles, crocodiles, and snakes are other types of reptiles.

Alligators are related to crocodiles. The two look very similar, but they each belong in their own family of reptiles.

The scales of an alligator look like a suit of armor.

Compare and Contrast

Seeing an American alligator in the wild is much more common than seeing a Chinese alligator. Why might that be the case?

There are two species, or types, of alligator: the American alligator and the Chinese alligator. The American alligator is the larger of the two. Chinese alligators are very rare, meaning there are not many of them alive. They are considered an endangered species.

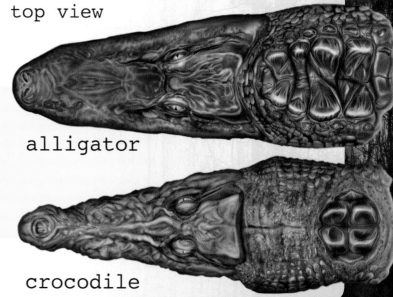

top view

alligator

crocodile

Viewed from above, it is easy to see differences between alligators (*top*) and crocodiles.

PHYSICAL FEATURES

Alligators are large lizardlike animals with long, rounded snouts and powerful tails. Male American alligators measure about 11 feet (3.4 meters) in length on average. The females are slightly smaller. Young American alligators are black with yellow stripes on the tail. Adults are brownish-black.

Alligators have many features in common with

Adult alligators have long black bodies without stripes.

Think About It

There are easy ways to tell alligators and crocodiles apart. One of the most obvious is that alligators have broad, rounded snouts, while most crocodiles have narrow, pointed snouts or noses.

crocodiles. They have thick skin composed of many scales and plates. They each have a long body and four short legs. The eyes, ears, and nostrils are located on top of the head. These show above the water when the animal floats.

Alligators are built so that they can still breathe, see, and hear when in the water.

ALLIGATOR BEHAVIOR

Alligators eat mainly fish, small mammals, and birds. Sometimes, they kill larger animals such as deer. Usually they hunt while underwater. They tend to swallow what they kill whole, without even chewing. Although they could eat a person, alligators tend to stay away from humans.

Alligators hunt in the water, snapping up food in their fierce jaws.

Compare and Contrast

In the wild, most alligators live to be about 50 years old. When kept in zoos or wildlife parks, they have lived for 70 years or more. Why might captivity help an animal live longer?

Alligators usually mate during the spring. The female builds a nest of mud and grass. She lays 20 to 60 white eggs in the nest. The eggs hatch after about 65 days. Young alligators live with their mother for as long as a year.

Newborn baby alligators face many dangers from other animals in the outside world.

PLACES GATORS CALL HOME

Chinese alligators are smaller and lighter-colored than American alligators.

American alligators live in the southeastern United States, especially Florida. Chinese alligators live in the Yangtze River region in China.

Almost every place on Earth—from the hottest desert to the coldest ice pack—is a habitat, or home, for animals and plants. Water habitats may contain freshwater or salt

Think About It

Alligators have a strong sense of where their home is. Scientists have discovered that they can return home even after they have been moved hundreds of miles away.

water. Freshwater habitats include streams, rivers, swamps, marshes, ponds, and lakes.

Alligators almost always live in freshwater habitats. They live along the edges of swamps, lakes, and slow-moving rivers. They spend most of their time in the water, but they also travel on land.

A grassy bank along a freshwater source is a likely place to spot an alligator.

HOW ANIMALS BECOME ENDANGERED

An endangered species is one that might become extinct, or disappear forever. Animals depend on their **environment** to survive. When their habitat changes or disappears, plants and animals may become endangered.

Sometimes, nature can harm an animal's home. Natural

An alligator rests in a small pool of water in the Florida Everglades.

Vocabulary

An **environment** is all of the living and nonliving things that surround a plant or animal.

disasters such as floods, hurricanes, and forest fires can harm or destroy habitats. New species might move into a habitat and threaten those that already live there.

Humans can cause species to become endangered as well. Humans pollute habitats with garbage, car fumes, and factory waste. They destroy habitats by clearing land for roads, buildings, and farms. They also may hunt and kill too many of certain types of animals.

Alligators need protection from a number of threats to their habitat.

ALLIGATORS IN DANGER

By the early 1960s, there were not many American alligators left in the wild. Hunting was a big reason why.

For years, alligators had been overhunted. An alligator's hide, meaning its skin made of scales, had been a popular material for purses, belts, and shoes.

Many alligator lives were lost for fashion statements such as these boots.

Think About It

Animals in danger are at first called "threatened." If nothing is done to help them, they may go from threatened to endangered. The next stop is extinction.

Some hunters killed alligators for their meat. Large numbers of young alligators were also sold as pets.

Hunting alligators, either to make money from their hides or for sport, was outlawed in the United States in 1962. In 1967, the American alligator was listed as an endangered species under the Endangered Species Preservation Act of 1966.

A photo from 1956 shows Native Americans capturing an alligator, before hunting reptiles became illegal.

HABITAT THREATS

An alligator lurks in an unspoiled section of the Florida Everglades.

Alligators have also faced the destruction of their habitats. This is especially true in the Florida Everglades.

The Everglades is a huge marsh, or area of wet land, that covers much of southern Florida. Warm weather and lots of water make this area a great habitat for many animal species. The Everglades are home to many American alligators.

Think About It

The Everglades is the only place where the American crocodile and the American alligator live peacefully together.

In some places, the Everglades have been drained to create farms and houses. Marsh water has also been changed to provide drinking water for humans and prevent city flooding. Pollution has widely ruined the land and water. Damage from hurricanes has made a lot of the Everglades unlivable for alligators as well.

Hurricane Andrew in 1992 destroyed parts of south Florida, including the alligator's habitat.

CONSERVATION TO THE RESCUE

Conservation is the protection of things found in nature. It requires the sensible use of all Earth's natural resources: water, soil, minerals, wildlife, and forests. People who care about conservation try to **preserve** natural resources so they will still be around in the future. They also try to keep the environment clean and healthy.

NATURAL AREA
CAUTION: Please stay on the path. This area contains sensitive natural habitats with some unstable land, surfaces, alligators, venomous snakes and stinging insects.

Keeping animal habitats in their natural state is a chief conservation goal.

Vocabulary

Preserve means to protect or to keep something from being lost or ruined.

Some resources are renewable, which means they can be replaced. Living things, such as plants and animals, are examples of renewable resources because they can reproduce themselves. But renewable resources can still be damaged or destroyed.

In the 1960s, people became more aware that many species were endangered, including the American alligator. Knowing about the problem made them want to do something to help.

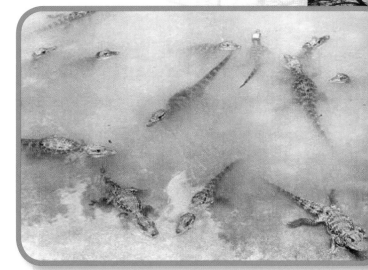

Young alligators swimming in tanks, away from harm, in Panama.

PROTECTED BY LAW

At first, American alligators were protected by the United States government through the Endangered Species Preservation Act. This law, passed in 1966, helped create programs aimed at protecting certain endangered animals.

Congress passed a stronger law, the Endangered Species Act, in 1973. This law covered

American alligators are making a comeback, thanks, in part, to the U.S. government.

Compare and Contrast

The Endangered Species Act included protection of an animal's habitat. Why do you think the government added this measure to the later law?

more animals and added protection for habitats as well. It also made it illegal to kill endangered animals or remove them from their natural habitat.

Scientists give a lot of the credit for saving the American alligator to the Endangered Species Act. The bald eagle and the gray wolf were also helped by this law.

Laws have made sure that alligators remain safe in their natural habitats.

VICTORY!

Overseeing alligator nests is one way to conserve the species.

Thanks to the Endangered Species Act and similar laws passed in individual states, alligators are no longer considered an endangered species. The number of American alligators in the wild has grown steadily since the 1970s. The conservation group Defenders of American Wildlife believes there are about five million American alligators living in the wild.

Vocabulary

Alligators are hatched, meaning they come out of eggs. That is why baby alligators are called hatchlings.

In addition to the laws protecting alligators, there are also programs that have helped increase their numbers. On alligator farms, nests are protected until the **hatchlings** can be set free in the wild. Alligator habitats have been preserved, too. In 2000, the United States government created a plan to help the Everglades return to its natural state. Beginning in 2009, water has been pumped back into the Florida marsh.

More baby alligators being born means less chance of extinction for the species.

GROUPS KEEPING WATCH

Many organizations worldwide work to keep endangered species from becoming extinct. The International Union for Conservation of Nature and Natural Resources keeps lists of endangered species. The Nature Conservancy and the World Wildlife Fund help to set aside land for threatened wildlife.

The Nature Conservancy opened Florida's Disney Wilderness Preserve in the early 1990s.

Compare and Contrast

International groups have helped protect American alligators. Why would people from other countries care about animals that live only in the United States?

Nature preserves and zoos help endangered animals to reproduce. Such programs have helped to increase the populations of some endangered animals, including the American alligator.

In the United States, the US Fish and Wildlife Service protects endangered and threatened wildlife. The service also works to conserve plant and animal habitats. The National Wildlife Federation and the federal government's Environmental Protection Agency also protect natural habitats.

The number of alligators keeps growing, thanks to conservation groups and caring individuals.

FUTURE RISKS?

American alligators are rebounding, but they are not totally out of the woods yet.

Alligator hunting is legal again in the United States. However, there are limits to how many may be captured or killed. Limits are **enforced** by the U.S. Fish and Wildlife Service.

Although they are no longer endangered, American alligators are still listed as threatened. Alligators look like certain endangered species, especially

Vocabulary

Enforced means making sure that rules and laws are followed.

the American crocodile. The government does not want people mistakenly killing crocodiles while hunting alligators. Making alligators threatened gives the government more control over how wild alligators are treated.

The main threat to American alligators today is damage to their habitats. Yet as long as people are aware and take steps to protect these creatures and their homes, alligators should be a nonendangered species for years to come.

Saving alligators from extinction is a very worthy cause.

GLOSSARY

CAPTIVITY The state of being held in one place and not being free.

EXTINCT No longer existing.

HABITAT The place where an animal or plant naturally lives or grows.

HATCH To be born by coming out of an egg.

NOSTRILS The openings of a nose through which an animal gets air.

POLLUTE To make dirty and unsafe for healthy living.

PRESERVATION To keep something in its original state or good condition.

RARE Uncommon, or hardly ever found.

RENEWABLE Able to be replaced or made new again naturally.

REPTILE A cold-blooded animal with scales or another hard covering.

SCALES Flat, hard plates that cover and protect an animal or fish.

SENSIBLE Having the ability to make good decisions.

SNOUT The long nose of certain animals.

SPECIES A group of animals or plants that are similar or related.

WASTE Garbage or other material not used and thrown away.

Books

Baxter, Bethany. *Caimans, Gharials, Alligators, and Crocodiles*. New York, NY: Rosen Publishing, 2014.

Gibbons, Gail. *Alligators and Crocodiles*. New York, NY: Holiday House, 2010.

Kalman, Bobbie. *The ABCs of Endangered Animals*. New York, NY: Crabtree Publishing Company, 2009.

Marsh, Laura. *National Geographic Readers: Alligators and Crocodiles*. Washington, DC: National Geographic Society, 2015.

Slade, Suzanne. *What Can We Do About Endangered Animals?* New York, NY: Rosen Publishing, 2010.

Spilsbury, Richard, and Louise Spilsbury. *Animals in Danger in North America*. Chicago, IL: Heinemann, 2013.

Websites

Because of the changing nature of Internet links, Rosen Publishing has developed an online list of websites related to the subject of this book. This site is updated regularly. Please use this link to access the list:

http://www.rosenlinks.com/CONS/Alli

INDEX